# Stres

# and Mood Boosters
# For Kids

How to help kids ease anxiety,
feel happy, and reach their goals!

## Jed Jurchenko

**www.CoffeeShopConversations.com**

© 2017 by Jed Jurchenko

Dedicated to parents, stepparents, foster parents, teachers, mentors, and coaches who tirelessly build into the lives of kids.

Dedicated to children and tweens who are in the process of learning how to bust stress and boost their mood as they patiently pursue their goals.

Dedicated to my own children, Mackenzie, Brooklyn, Addison, and Emmalynn.

Your love for life is contagious!

May your adventuresome spirits and creativity continue to grow.

# Also by Jed

**131 Conversations that Engage Kids**

**131 Boredom Busters and Creativity Builders**

**131 Creative Conversations for Couples**

**131 Engaging Conversations for Couples**

**131 Creative Conversations for Families**

**131 Necessary Conversations before Marriage**

**131 Conversations for Stepfamily Success**

**Ten Quick Wins for Writers**

**Coffee Shop Conversations:
Psychology and the Bible**

**Coffee Shop Inspirations:
Simple Strategies for Building Dynamic
Leadership and Relationships**

# Get the Free Workbook!

**Dive deeper with the *131 Stress Busters and Mood Boosters Workbook!***

This printable workbook is packed with activities that encourage kids to bust stress and boost their mood.

Activities Include:

- Conversation Cards
- Self-Regulation Word Searches
- Coping Skills Fortuneteller Activity
- Self-Talk Mazes and more

Download your free workbook at:

www.CoffeeShopConversations.com/BustStress

# Contents

# The Power of Self-Regulation

Children who can self-regulate have higher odds of excelling virtually everywhere. Parents who teach their kids to bust stress, boost their mood, and persistently press forward toward their goals not only pass on an invaluable skill but also equip their children to win at life. Thanks to Professor Walter Mischel and his team of Stanford University graduate students, there is ample evidence supporting this.

In the 1960s, Professor Mischel began researching how preschoolers manage stress. He created an experiment that took place in an area dubbed *The Surprise Room,* and data was collected from over six hundred four-, five-, and six-year-old children. Furnished with only a table and chair (and equipped with a panel of two-way glass to conceal the presence of the research team), *The Surprise Room* was intentionally distraction free.

In this space, Walter's tiny participants played a game that put their ability to self-regulate to the test. One by one, each child was ushered into the room, seated at the table, and asked to select a small treat. Because children often chose a marshmallow, the experiment eventually became known as *The Marshmallow Experiment.*

Each child was offered a simple choice. He or she could devour a single marshmallow now or enjoy two marshmallows later. The only catch was the child would have to wait an entire fifteen minutes to receive the additional reward. The researcher then placed the marshmallow on the table and exited the room.

Having the sweet indulgence within arm's reach created a stressful situation for the child and ideal conditions for Walter's research. Could these kids defend against temptation? What skills would they use to resist the enticing treats? This is precisely what Walter and his team wanted to know.

As you can imagine, some children gulped down the marshmallow immediately. Others held out for a few minutes before relenting. Out of the children who attempted to wait, only one in three managed to hold out the entire fifteen minutes. Although the study itself is fascinating, the research gathered over the following decades is what makes this experiment truly extraordinary. Over the next forty years, Walter's team remained in contact with their original participants, amassing as much information about their lives as possible.

The results are astounding. Children who waited to eat the marshmallow as preschoolers grew up to have "higher SAT scores, lower levels of substance abuse, a lower likelihood of obesity, better responses to stress, better social skills as reported by their parents, and generally better scores in a range of other life measures."[1] This includes higher self-reported levels of happiness, fewer instances of divorce, and higher rates of relationship satisfaction. In short, children who waited to eat the marshmallow were winning at life!

Today, Walter's work is highly regarded. It is taught in psychology courses and is the subject of popular Ted Talks, books, and internet articles. Duplicate experiments have even been uploaded to YouTube.[2] Undoubtedly, this simple test resonates with people profoundly.

## AVOIDING LIFE'S MARSHMALLOWS

So why are adults attracted to this study like a child to a marshmallow? I believe it is because nearly everyone can relate to the struggles of waiting and to the ecstasy of reaching one's goal. At first glance, connecting adult success with a single childhood decision not to gulp down a marshmallow may seem overly simplistic. However, upon closer examination, this correlation makes sense.

Obviously, *The Marshmallow Experiment* is not about the marshmallow. Children who waited to eat the treat went on to excel, not due to their capacity to avoid sugar but because of their ability to assert effortful control over their lives. In other words, when these kids needed to delay gratification to reach their objective, they could. Whether this quality is called effortful control, patient persistence, grit, or self-regulation, the same set of skills applies. The common factors include:

1. Being able to reduce one's level of stress so as not to be overwhelmed by frustrations.

2. The ability to make oneself reasonably happy in the moment.

11

3.  The capacity to keep going until the goal is attained.

## EVERYDAY MARSHMALLOWS

To better understand the significance of these skills, let's examine some examples of real-life marshmallows that kids face:

- Watching television instead of completing chores.

- Guzzling soda and junk foods to the detriment of a balanced diet.

- Playing video games and electronics instead of studying for a test.

- Chatting with friends late into the evening as opposed to getting a full night's rest.

- Avoiding a daily regimen of brushing and flossing because it feels like too much work.

- Refusing to share one's toys with friends because this is more appealing at the moment.

These common childhood traps shed light on why self-regulation matters. Imagine how much better life could be for your child if he or she were able to remain reasonably content while completing difficult but important tasks.

## MARSHMALLOW-AVOIDING ADULTS

*The Marshmallow Study* reveals that marshmallow-resisting children grow up to become marshmallow-resisting adults. Self-regulation is like riding a bike. Although challenging at first, once mastered, the ability sticks for life.

As children transition into adulthood, the capacity to manage negative emotions in a positive way becomes even more advantageous. Illustrations of this include the self-regulating employee who puts personal drama on pause so he can fully engage at work. This makes it far more likely that he will receive a raise. Self-regulated couples set aside their differences to connect, which increases their odds of a happy, healthy, lasting relationship. One example of this is the husband who chooses to record a sporting event and attend the opera with his wife, even though he does not particularly enjoy opera. This wise husband knows that making time for his spouse is far more important than any game.

Do you get the picture? The ability to remain positive while steadily pursuing one's aspirations makes all the difference. The next logical question is "How do parents nurture this quality in their kids?" or more playfully stated, "How do parents help children circumvent life's marshmallows?"

## MASTERING THE ART OF COPING

Marshmallow-avoiding children are not born with magical abilities. In fact, it is fascinating to note that many of the skills observed by Walter and his team were unsophisticated and even downright gross. Yet, the strategies worked.

So how did these future successes of the world make waiting easier? They distracted themselves by sticking their fingers in their nose, mouth, and ears, exploring every orifice of their face—disgusting for sure! They sat on their hands, rendering themselves physically incapable of yielding to temptation—a simple strategy that also happened to be exactly what that child needed in the moment. Other children hummed,

14

sang, distracted themselves with finger play, pushed the delicacy away, attempted to fall asleep, covered their eyes, and turned their back toward the treat.

Avoiding marshmallows is not rocket science. Basic stress-management skills allowed these children to reach their goal, which makes me wonder if equipping children with the skills to succeed might be easier than we think.

Therapists refer to these strategies as coping skills. All successful people, regardless of their age, title, or stage of life, have an arsenal of positive coping skills at their disposal. However, the application of these skills often looks quite different. For instance, the marathon runner who pushes through the pain by mentally repeating, *Running is simply placing one foot in front of the other*, is employing a positive coping skill to finish the race. The department store employee who takes a deep breath, smiles, and says, "Yes, I can see you are frustrated, and I will do my best to help," when confronted by an irate customer, is also using a healthy coping skill.

On a personal level, there are moments when writing is so exasperating that tossing my laptop off the balcony in a fit of frustration would feel especially gratifying. However, when I instead choose to pause for a break by walking to the refrigerator, pouring a cold glass of water, and then returning to the task at hand, I too am putting coping skills to work.

## EQUIPPING CHILDREN TO WIN

This book provides an arsenal of coping skills to help children bust stress, boost their mood, and patiently pursue their goals. When practiced consistently, this pattern leads to success. And it works in virtually every area of life! Because coping skills develop over time, teaching, modeling, and practicing these skills with your kids on a consistent basis is especially important. In short, taking action is far more valuable than merely knowing what one should do.

In the pages ahead, you will find 131 stress-busting, mood-boosting coping skills. Your job is to teach them to your children and to reinforce them at every opportunity you get. Doing this will embed these skills in your child's memory and make them his or her automatic response to stress. The best time to teach these coping skills is now. Fortunately, one is never too young or too old to implement the ideas in this book.

## HELPING KIDS COPE

From the moment a child is born, parents help their kids learn how to cope. A crying baby, who is nursed, changed, and gently soothed to sleep, is taught to seek support from others—a skill that will serve him well for the rest of his life. As children mature, they develop the ability to apply increasingly complex skills, such as stacking coping skills together. This strategy is expanded upon in later chapters.

My simple definition of a coping skill is *any healthy strategy that allows a child to feel good enough to persist.* I like the phrase "good enough," because it highlights a balanced approach. Contrary to what some self-help gurus suggest, it is not necessary to feel elated all the time. This would be exhausting. Instead, the aim is to prevent negative emotions from taking over. Sometimes life is hard. No skills will change this. The ideas in this book do, however, assist children in persisting through challenges without becoming overwhelmed in the process.

## EUSTRESS AND DISTRESS

Cars need oil changes, computers require restarts, and the human body must have rest. This is true even during happy times. According to psychology, there are two types of stress. Distresses are events that feel bad. Common childhood distresses include failing a test, losing a longstanding friendship, and completing chores at home.

However, stress also comes in sneakier forms. *Eustress* is a term that describes positive life events that contribute to stress buildup. For adults, getting married, buying a house, or receiving a promotion at work are all eustress events, as these activities are amazing and emotionally taxing at the same time.

For children, moving to a new home (even if the new one is nicer), switching schools, making new friends, becoming the star player on a sports team, and reaching major milestones contribute to eustress buildup. Stressors, both good and bad, big and small, are everywhere and frequently go unnoticed. Because stress is cumulative, it has a knack of sneaking up and overwhelming kids.

## KIDS, STRESS, AND GUNPOWDER

Stress is like a barrel of gunpowder. When kids stuff stress inside, it accumulates and packs tight. Eventually, a tiny upset sparks an immense explosion. The child's outburst might manifest in a fit of anger, a river of tears, or in the child giving up. Whenever an emotional outburst is far greater than the situation warrants, stress buildup is usually involved.

Fortunately, self-regulation skills allow children to release their gunpowder-like stress and avoid the explosion. Using coping skills throughout the day is similar to sprinkling a barrel of gunpowder over a large parking lot. When ignited, instead of a "BOOM," there is only a sizzle and a "poof." No damage is done because the stress was released over time.

## REST FOR SUCCESS

Life sends ongoing barrages of stressors our kid's way. Because of this, it is essential that children learn to establish consistent rhythms of rest. When your child's first reaction to a negative event is to take a deep breath and remind herself she is capable of handling the difficulty, then you have done your job well.

Recently a manager friend expressed her disappointment at the number of job applicants who missed their interviews. She remarked, "Sometimes I think 50 percent of success comes from just showing up." I would agree and expand on this wisdom. In my opinion, roughly 90 percent of success results from showing up consistently and completing the task at hand while maintaining a positive attitude in the process.

Although this percentage is only an assumption, I think most people will agree. The ability to regulate one's emotions and press forward until a goal is achieved is the most basic recipe for success. This is what allowed a handful of preschoolers to avoid eating the marshmallow, and according to the research, it is what will allow your child to triumph in nearly every area of life.

# Why Coping Skills Work

Coping skills prevent kids from losing their minds and behaving like animals. Without them, children act impulsively, saying things they do not mean and hurting those they love. While this may sound like an odd statement, it is based on biological research. Let me further explain with a story.

It was the end of a gorgeous fall day. The sun was setting as our family traveled home from our annual apple-picking excursion in the quaint town of Julian. Little did we know that we had one more adventure in store. I was behind the wheel of our family's white minivan. My wife, Jenny, sat next to me, chatting about the events of the day, while our four children happily hunkered down with books and movies in the back.

After traversing a bend in the road, I spotted a fully-grown mountain lion peering out from the woods. In San Diego, a mountain lion sighting is a rare occurrence, so my initial reaction was excitement. However, as I enthusiastically encouraged my family to look out the windows, something alarming occurred. The beast bolted into the road, froze in the center of our lane, and gave us an icy glare.

A flood of questions whirled through my mind. *If I slam on the breaks, will I be rear-ended by the car behind us? Is it safe to stop this close to a mountain lion? Will my family be injured if our vehicle collides with the beast?*

The next few seconds felt like an eternity. Lacking clear direction, I eased my foot on the breaks—slowing but not stopping our vehicle—and hoped for the best. Sensing the oncoming danger, the mountain lion scrambled into the woods. Regrettably, he was not quite fast enough. Our slowing minivan gingerly clipped his hindquarters as he sped away. Luckily, no lasting damage was done. However, that mountain lion will undoubtedly think twice before attempting to stare down another vehicle.

## PANIC-BUTTON PROBLEMS

I share this story because it illustrates how a tiny part of the brain can hijack one's ability to think critically. So why did that mountain lion unexpectedly bolt into the road? According to psychology, this animal took flight, froze, prepared to fight, and then took flight again for the same reason people do. His amygdala hijacked his brain. The amygdala is the brain's crude emergency response system that can be both a help and a hindrance. In other words, everyone has panic-button problems.

When people are triggered, similar to a spooked mountain lion, they act in irrationally impulsive ways. The amygdala is what causes a couple who is deeply in love to argue bitterly, to the point of scarring their relationship for life. It is why children break their favorite toys during temper tantrums and drop out of activities they love after experiencing a minor setback.

This tiny, almond-shaped portion of the brain is responsible for the fight, flight, or freeze reactions in our bodies. Although these primal instincts are a lifesaver in genuine emergencies, they stir up chaos during false alarms. To understand how this works, picture the amygdala and the frontal cortex—or the critical thinking part of the brain—connected by a switch. When one turns on, the other turns off. This means that when the amygdala activates, clear and rational thinking is nearly impossible.

To drive this point home, one of my favorite college professors refers to the amygdala as "Amy G. Dala." This personification keenly portrays the hijacking power of this tiny mass of gray matter. Amy G. is highly emotional. She does not think but simply acts. Sensing danger as our vehicle approached, Amy G. ordered the mountain lion to take flight. Unfortunately, Amy G. is fickle. She quickly changed her mind, deciding that freezing then fighting would be better. Fortunately, before a head-on collision ensued, Amy G. commanded the mountain lion to resume its flight.

As one would expect, Amy G. wreaks havoc when critical thinking is required. Relationships are where she does her most damage. Close connections are something that Amy G. knows little about. Unfortunately, this does not deter her from getting involved, which is precisely why equipping kids with tools to avert Amy G.'s influence is so important.

## AMY G. AND YOUR CHILD

In a crisis, such as a fire, burglary, or earthquake, Amy G. passionately strives to keep children safe. She pushes them to run, take cover, hide, and fight back. While this can be a good thing, Amy G.'s trigger-happy nature is not. Her motto is "better safe than sorry," and she is ready to shut down a child's frontal cortex at the first sign of danger.

Sadly, Amy G. does not recognize the seriousness of the consequences that result. Children who are emotionally triggered will act in ways that are out of character. For instance, a typically gentle child may become verbally aggressive, rageful, or violent. A normally caring individual might shut down, isolate, or boldly proclaim that he or she no longer cares at all. When a rational child acts recklessly during emotionally charged circumstances, Amy G. is usually involved.

## SOOTHING AMY G.

The first reason the strategies in this book work is because they soothe Amy G. When a child notices feelings of panic welling up inside and pauses to take a deep breath, the amygdala relaxes. This allows the frontal cortex to remain in control, which drastically increases the odds of a positive outcome.

The amygdala is sometimes referred to as "the reptilian brain," and it is easy to see why. Even lizards know how to fight, freeze, and take flight. A basic key to success is continually thinking at a higher level than a reptile. Children who are able to prevent Amy G. from taking charge of non-emergency situations have fewer temper outbursts, emotional shutdowns, and moments of despair. Thus, they are better equipped to handle life.

## DRAINING TOXIC STRESS

A second reason the strategies in this book work is because they alleviate stress before it turns toxic. Contrary to popular belief, not all stress is bad. Because of this, the goal is not to eliminate stress but to equip kids with tools for managing it in healthy ways.

Interestingly, there are three different types of stress. The first is healthy stress, a powerful motivator that leads to mastering new skills, achieving goals, and seeking help from others. Healthy stress is beneficial because a completely stress-free life would also be an unmotivated life. From a practical standpoint, healthy stress pushes children to complete homework assignments, practice before a big game, and act responsibly at home. In limited doses, stress provides children with an extra push to complete difficult but essential tasks.

The second level of stress is tolerable stress. Tolerable stress is an increasing pressure that leads to anxiety. A child who wakes up in a panic because he did not practice the school presentation due that day will experience tolerable stress. Although this type of stress feels bad, it does not cause lasting damage.

The final and most severe level of stress is toxic stress. Toxic stress results from prolonged activation of the amygdala. According to neuroscience, a continually heightened state of arousal will eventually alter the brain's architecture. In other words, toxic stress causes the amygdala to take over. This leads to a diminished capacity for critical thinking that becomes the new norm.

## TOXIC STRESS AND MENTAL ILLNESS

With this in mind, it is not surprising to learn that toxic stress leads to mental illness. According to the diathesis-stress model of mental illness, it is possible for people to drive themselves crazy—literally! The term *diathesis* refers to a genetic propensity for mental illness present in everyone. Some children are especially susceptible to depression. Others are more prone to anxiety, oppositional defiant disorders, schizophrenia, or bipolar disorder. When a person's level of stress elevates above the threshold that they can bear, the symptoms of mental illness kick in, amplifying with increased and prolonged exposure.

## ELIMINATING TOXIC BUILD-UP

Stress is cumulative. What begins as tolerable stress can turn toxic. Dealing with toxic stress is not this book's goal, as this is best accomplished under the guidance of a skilled therapist. Instead, the aim is to help children prevent healthy stress and tolerable stress from reaching toxic levels.

One way stress turns toxic is when children hone-in on their worries. This causes problems to feel bigger than they truly are and leads to feeling worse. Albert Ellis, the founder of Rational Emotive Behavioral Therapy, refers to this as *awfulizing* and *catastrophizing*.

Poor coping also increases the toxicity of stress. For instance, eating an entire pan of brownies produces an initial high that ends in a new low once the sugar hangover kicks in. The next chapter provides positive alternative strategies that help kids avoid these toxic traps.

## BURSTING THE HAPPINESS MYTH

Finally, the strategies in this book help children feel happier. The idea that self-care is selfish is a myth. Children who practice healthy self-care not only boost their mood, they also provide an amazing gift to others. Moods are highly contagious, and when your child is happy, everyone they meet will share in this joy. If you doubt this, the next time a baby smiles at you, I challenge you to try not smiling back. Thanks to *mirror neurons*, this is practically impossible.

Let me further explain. In the early 1990s, a team of Italian researchers discovered mirror neurons, or neurons that fire when one human being detects an emotion in another. This means that the act of observing someone else smile actually causes the observer to feel happier. People literally share in the joy of others. For this reason, when children attend to their happiness needs, they lift the moods of everyone they meet.

## WHY HAPPINESS MATTERS

One of my favorite quotes comes from Ray Tucker. Ray states, "There are two types of leaders, those who generate energy and those who consume energy. Be a leader who generates energy." To fit with the theme of this book, I would tweak this to proclaim, "There are two types of kids, those who spread happiness and those who consume happiness. Help your kids to bust stress, boost their mood, and spread joy to everyone they meet!" Parents who help their children accomplish this endow them with an extraordinary skill that benefits them for the rest of their life!

Now, that we have examined how these stress-busting and mood-boosting skills work, it is time to take action. I wish you and your kids much success as you begin the journey ahead.

# 131 Stress Busters and Mood Boosters

You're braver than you believe,
and stronger than you seem,
and smarter than you think.

*~Christopher Robin*


Courage is not the absence of fear,
but doing something in spite of fear.

*~Unknown*


Don't underestimate the value
of doing nothing, of just going along,
listening to all the things you can't hear,
and not bothering.

*~Winnie the Pooh*

## BREATHE DEEPLY

"Take a deep breath, and calm down." You have likely heard this advice before and, perhaps, have even given it yourself. Even so, this simple strategy is worth repeating, because breathing deeply works. Whether you are a 2-year-old or 102, filling your lungs to capacity then gradually releasing the air is a foundational way of preventing an amygdala hijacking from occurring.

I have taught this skill to adults as part of a fifty-two-week domestic violence offenders program. I have also used a bubble-wand and a pinwheel to practice this skill with toddlers. So why does this strategy work? Taking a deep breath oxygenates the brain, slows the body down, and provides additional time for children to think.

When kids are upset, quick and shallow breathing is the norm. This increases anxiety and prepares the body to react. I sometimes tell the impulsive teenagers I see, "It's awesome that we get to meet now before any lasting damage is done. Our goal is to help you to avoid bigger mistakes in the future and the consequences that come with them."

The first six strategies in this book help kids to improve their mood by taking slow, deep breaths. Although this skill is simple, it is surprisingly potent. Thus, encouraging kids to practice taking deep breaths, to the point it becomes second nature, is highly recommended.

## Buster & Booster #1

Take a big, deep breath.

> Inhale through your nose and exhale through your mouth. When kids find themselves amid tense situations, this is also the perfect time for them to step away and reorient before deciding what to do next.

## Buster & Booster #2

Blow a pinwheel, and see how long you can keep the wheel spinning.

## Buster & Booster #3

Blow bubbles.

## Buster & Booster #4

Blow feathers.

> Kids can cup their hands together and blow the feathers out or propel a single feather across a tabletop.

## Buster & Booster #5

Take elephant breaths.

> Stand with your feet apart, body bent slightly forward, and arms dangling in front of you like an elephant's trunk. Slowly breathe in through your nose. As you do, raise your body and extend your arms until you are standing straight, with your arms fully raised above your head. As you exhale through your mouth, gradually return to your original position.

## Buster & Booster #6

Go for a swim.

Not only is swimming excellent exercise but it is also a fantastic way for kids to learn how to control their breathing.

# BE FULLY PRESENT

According to *The Worry Cure*, worrying is normal. In fact, worrying is so common that roughly 35 percent of people engage in it daily.[3] However, because 85 percent of the things people worry about never happen, worrying is mostly worthless. More importantly, studies reveal that when bad things do ensue, 79 percent of the time they are not as bad as expected, or the situation is managed better than anticipated. This means that 97 percent of the time, worry only creates unnecessary misery.

When children worry, they are physically secure, but their mind becomes trapped in a negative past or future event. It is important to note there is nothing wrong with some anxiety. In limited doses, this is a normal, healthy, and motivating emotion. However, when children get stuck in worry, the resulting anxiety can become debilitating.

This next set of stress busters and mood boosters helps children return their focus to the present. After all, this is the only place they can be truly happy. Also, since the majority of what kids worry about never transpires, worrying is simply not worth the effort.

## Buster & Booster #7

Use the 5-4-3-2-1 technique to return to the present moment.

Kids can do this by identifying five things they see, four things they hear, three things they feel (e.g., the solid ground beneath their feet, the soft clothes they are wearing, the wind against their face), two things they smell, and one thing they taste.

## Buster & Booster #8

Splash cool water on your face.

The slight change in temperature, coupled with the sensory experience, helps children return to the here and now.

## Buster & Booster #9

Squeeze an ice cube.

> This coping skill packs a double-whammy, as the squeezing of the fist and the cold of the ice take the focus away from problems and on to the present moment.

## Buster & Booster #10

Sit with the pain and experience it fully.

> Strong emotions do not last forever, and sometimes the quickest way to the other side is straight through. Because our emotional response system is not designed to remain under duress for long, when a child sits with the pain, the intensity of the feelings will dissipate. This tool is not appropriate for every child, but under the right circumstances, it can work well.

## Buster & Booster #11

Draw a picture of your anger, fear, sadness, or frustration.

> This helps children to understand better what they are feeling. Then talk about the picture, listen empathetically, and assure your child that he or she is safe at this moment.

## Buster & Booster #12

Schedule a time to be upset later.

> For example, schedule ten minutes of worry at 5 p.m. When the set time rolls around, some kids will find they no longer need it. Other children will want to stick to the schedule. In this case, children discover they have some ability to manage their emotions.

## Buster & Booster #13

Allow yourself five minutes to be upset now.

> This strategy is perfect for children who are unable to wait. Simply set a timer and allow your child time to vent. Listen empatheti-

cally. Provide comfort in the moment. Then, after the timer dings, shift into the present moment, where life is good. This is another excellent way to help children increase their emotional control.

# CHANGE YOUR TEMPERATURE

Every year, I teach a general psychology class where the textbook teaches that temperature influences mood.[4] Did you know that more acts of violence occur during the heat of the summer months? Fortunately, a chilly drink or cool shower can help soothe anger on a sweltering day.

Similarly, a warm bath or a cozy drink on a frosty day can cause the world to feel brighter. This next set of stress busters and mood boosters demonstrates how to use changes in temperature to help your child self-regulate.

## Buster & Booster #14

Sip a tall glass of ice water, lemonade, or another chilly drink.

## Buster & Booster #15

Take a cool shower.

## Buster & Booster #16

Place a cold washcloth on your forehead.

## Buster & Booster #17

Sip hot tea, apple cider, or cocoa.

## Buster & Booster #18

Take a warm bath.

Add bubbles or a few drops of lavender oil for an additional calming effect.

## ACT HAPPY

An easy way for a child to feel happier is to act happier. Psychology teaches that we are biopsychosocial beings. This complex term describes how biology, psychology, and social interactions intertwine to influence moods and actions. *Biology* refers to the chemical makeup of our physical bodies. *Psychology* encompasses our thoughts and mental process, and the word *social* describes our interpersonal interactions.

The interconnectedness of my biology, psychology, and social relationships became clear during my junior year of high school. "Ok, let's try this again. I would like you to hold your hand palm-down and keep it as steady as possible." Yet it was no use. The sheet of notebook paper the doctor placed on my hand shook vehemently before drifting to the floor.

"Well, this explains a lot," the doctor exclaimed. "The reason you can't hold your hand still is because your heart is racing at 120 beats a minute. As you sit in my office, your heart is running a marathon."

I left the doctor's office diagnosed with Graves Disease, also known as a hyperactive thyroid. Somewhere toward the end of middle school, this tiny gland in my neck malfunctioned. This change in my biology created a chain reaction that also altered my thoughts and friendships.

I remember the balmy San Diego days where I would sweat profusely and struggle to stay focused in class, even though my peers seemed just fine. As you can imagine, my racing heart led to slipping grades, which caused me to think, *I am no good at school.* As a result, I adjusted my social interactions to fit my perceived identity by increasing my associations with slackers, underachievers, and the kids who didn't care. *After all,* I told myself, *this is where I belong.*

By the time my junior year in high school rolled around, I was a train wreck. Fortunately, a wise doctor helped me get back on track. All it took was a simple medication that brought my biology back into balance. Soon my grades improved, as did my self-esteem and the quality of my relationships.

I share this story because it demonstrates how one's biology, psychology, and social interactions all intertwine. It also illustrates how a boost in one area can elevate the others. Adults can use this knowledge to their advantage by helping children understand that happy kids act happy.

The physical act of smiling increases cheerful thoughts and the odds that someone else will smile back. These things work together to stir up genuine feelings of happiness. In other words, when children act the part, the feelings eventually follow. This next set of mood boosters helps children to feel happier by acting happier.

## Buster & Booster #19

Smile. Better yet, look someone in the eyes and let a warm, gentle smile ease across your face.

According to psychology, the simple act of smiling makes one feel happier. I first discovered this principle in Dale Carnegie's classic, How to Win Friends and Influence People. Ever since, I have been pleasantly surprised at just how powerful this simple mood-boosting strategy is. Teach your kids to smile at family, friends, and peers they would like to meet. Not only will this brighten their day, chances are it will spread joy to those around them too.

## Buster & Booster #20

Listen to positive, upbeat music.

## Buster & Booster #21

Have a dance party.

> This is a personal family favorite that has led to a multitude of happy memories in our home.

## Buster & Booster #22

Watch a humorous movie or television show.

## Buster & Booster #23

Read inspirational quotes.

## Buster & Booster #24

Act like today will be amazing.

## Buster & Booster #25

Look back to past successes.

> As you do, remind yourself that you succeeded once and you can most certainly do it again!

## Buster & Booster #26

Act like the most optimistic person you know.

> First, visualize the happiest person you know. Then, try to borrow this person's mannerisms, facial expressions, and attitude. Remember, happy people act happy. Go about your day as if you were in a positive mood, and the feelings will eventually follow.

## Buster & Booster #27

Find an excuse to smile and laugh.

> Don't overthink this one. Any excuse will do.

## Buster & Booster #28

Skip.

## DRAW STRENGTH FROM FAITH

In the Bible, many of the psalms begin in despair and end in joy. The reason for this is that David, who authored much of this book, knew how to draw strength from his faith.

As a psychology professor at a seminary, I have discovered that people regularly hold the misconception that psychology and faith mix about as well as orange juice and toothpaste or screen doors on a submarine. However, this is simply not the case. In fact, *Psychology*, a general psychology textbook authored by David Myers, lists nurturing one's spiritual self as a primary way to feel happier.

Myers states, "People active in faith communities report greater-than-average happiness and often cope well with crisis."[4] Faith brings hope. Because of this, helping kids draw strength from their faith is an excellent way to support them in busting stress and boosting their mood. The next section provides ideas for accomplishing this.

## Buster & Booster #29

Pray.

## Buster & Booster #30

Ask a pastor, lay minister, Sunday school teacher, or friend to pray for you.

## Buster & Booster #31

Read a book of inspirational Scriptures.

## Buster & Booster #32

Sing along to worship music in the car.

> My daughter, Addison, loves to rock out to "God's Not Dead," by The Newsboys, during our drive to school. She sings with so much enthusiasm that I look forward to this daily ritual. Moreover, a college student I know describes using worship music to transform high-stress, traffic-filled commutes into her "Jesus party time." After implementing this change, she reports arriving at work energized and refreshed.

## Buster & Booster #33

Vent to God.

> Many of the psalms begin in sorrow and end in joy. David was a master at venting his frustrations to his Creator and leaving problems in God's hands.

## Buster & Booster #34

Read a kid's devotional book as a family.

## Buster & Booster #35

Share with your child how you draw strength from your faith.

> In 1 Corinthians 11:1, the apostle Paul writes, "Be imitators of me, just as I also am of Christ."[5] Wise adults teach children in a similar fashion. They live out their faith and inspire kids with their example.

## Buster & Booster #36

Seek wisdom from a pastor, Sunday school teacher, or church leader.

One is never too young nor too old to seek advice from others.

## PRACTICE GRATITUDE

When kids practice gratitude, the world feels brighter. Gratitude not only boosts one's physical and mental health but it also promotes an overall sense of wellbeing. In fact, gratitude's ability to lift one's spirits is so compelling that two researchers from the University of Miami, Robert Emmons and Michael McCullough, refer to it as "the forgotten factor in happiness research."[6]

During their study, Robert and Michael discovered that those who kept a weekly happiness journal exercised more often, had fewer adverse physical health symptoms, felt better about their lives, and were more optimistic than the control group (who only journaled about negative or neutral life events). In addition, those who practice gratitude daily are more likely to be a physical and emotional support to those in need.

Thus, gratitude is a powerful force that supercharges happiness. In regard to kids, it increases their energy, strengthens their relationships, and inspires them to support others. In a world bursting at the seams with entitled youth, many adults consider it a pleasure to be in the presence of a grateful adolescent.

However, helping children to appreciate the amazing things around them requires intentional effort. Gratitude is like a muscle; it develops with ongoing use. The next set of strategies hones in on ways adults can help kids bust stress and boost their mood by flexing their gratitude.

## Buster & Booster #37

For a quick mood boost, list ten things you are thankful for right now.

> To make this even more powerful, encourage children to enlist the help of family members and create a gratitude journal of 100 items or more. Not only is this an exciting challenge, an extended gratitude list is a powerful resource that children can refer back to during discouraging moments in their lives.

## Buster & Booster #38

Identify ten things that went well for you during the past week.

> "What is going well?" This is one of my favorite questions to ask the kids I meet with. I am a firm believer that there are always

positives in our children's lives. The trick is to find them. I have watched countless kids regain joy and rebuild momentum as they become aware of just how many positives they have.

## Buster & Booster #39

Mail a thank-you card.

## Buster & Booster #40

Send a thoughtful email or text with the goal of brightening someone else's day.

## Buster & Booster #41

Thank your grandparents, teacher, or coach for building into your life.

When you do this, get as specific as possible. Tell them exactly what you appreciate and why it is so meaningful to you. This can be accomplished in a letter, through a phone call, or in person.

## GET ACTIVE

According to psychology, aerobic exercise can alleviate mild depression and reduce anxiety. Of course, this is in addition to improving one's physical health and increasing mental clarity. Runners use the term *runner's high* to describe the pleasurable state that results from the body's release of natural endorphins. Moreover, being active is simply a whole lot of fun.

Personally, running is my cure for writer's block. This stress buster and mood booster always unlocks a vault of creativity. For some kids, being active comes naturally. Nevertheless, in today's high-tech world, others are sucked into the black hole of electronic devices. These kids will require extra motivation to get their bodies moving. This next section provides simple ways adults can inspire kids to increase their joy through physical activity.

### Buster & Booster #42

Take a walk.

## Buster & Booster #43

Go for a run.

## Buster & Booster #44

Hike.

## Buster & Booster #45

Throw a football.

## Buster & Booster #46

Play basketball.

> If no one is around to play with you, see how many free throws you can make in two minutes, play a solo game of Around the World, or set up a dribbling obstacle course.

## Buster & Booster #47

Do push-ups, crunches, lunges, or jumping jacks.

> Assist kids in putting together a simple exercise routine they can implement at home. Then encourage them to practice it three times a week or more.

## Buster & Booster #48

Jump rope.

> Try to get to 100 jumps without stopping.

## Buster & Booster #49

Bounce on a trampoline.

## Buster & Booster #50

Attend an aerobics class.

## Buster & Booster #51

Put on a children's exercise video and follow along.

## Buster & Booster #52

Go to the gym or YMCA, and keep your body moving.

# FIDGET

Fidgeting is a longstanding stress-relieving skill that is making a serious comeback. In 1996, during my senior year in high school, the *Tickle Me Elmo* doll was the hottest toy around. Stores could not keep them on the shelves, and scalpers were reportedly asking as much as $5,000 for the furry red monster.[7]

I remember thinking the Elmo craze was hilarious. However, last year, our youngest daughter received one of these nostalgic toys from her grandmother. After watching it in action, I have to admit the *Tickle Me Elmo* doll is cool. The point of this story is that fads catch on for a reason.

As I write this book, fidget spinners are the newest craze. It seems like every child carries at least two or three in their pockets at all times. Much to the dismay of adults, their familiar *whizzzzzzzzz* is heard in homes, classrooms, restaurants, parks, and shopping malls. Children cannot seem to get enough of this simple gadget. Yet, their popularity has a purpose. Children, as it turns out, have a profusion of excess energy.

With the reduction of physical education in schools and limits placed on the types of activities kids are allowed to play during recess—including bans on classic games like dodgeball and tag in some schools—it makes perfect sense that fidget spinners have caught on with a vengeance. Fortunately, these whirling plastic devices are not the only way for kids to release pent-up energy. The next set of stress busters and mood boosters provides simple fidgets that kids can use just about anywhere.

## Buster & Booster #53

Twiddle your thumbs by interlock the fingers of both hands and twirling your thumbs in a circle.

If this is too easy, switch things up by going in reverse too. I sometimes tell kids that this is the original fidget spinner.

## Buster & Booster #54

Squeeze your hands tightly together for a few seconds. Then relax and repeat.

> The physical act of tensing and relaxing is an excellent stress-relieving fidget. In class, kids can do this in a non-distracting manner by placing their hands underneath their desk and keeping their eyes directed toward the front of the room.

## Buster & Booster #55

Use a fidget cube or stress ball.

## Buster & Booster #56

Chew a stick of gum.

## Buster & Booster #57

Bounce your leg.

# CONNECT WITH YOUR EMOTIONS

Clarifying one's feelings and experiencing them to the fullest is often the fastest route to the other side. Yet accomplishing this can be tricky, as feelings are fickle and incredibly confusing. In the animated movie *Home*, Oh, a purple alien voiced by Jim Parsons, attempts to understand human emotions. Oh asks his human companion, "So, you are sad-mad?" This fictional alien understands something that many people do not. Human beings are capable of experiencing two or more emotions simultaneously.

This can be especially confusing for kids. Taking simple steps to identify the emotion or emotions involved brings clarity to the situation and serves as a starting point for generating solutions. This section also offers strategies for sitting with the pain, because sometimes the fastest way through a dark place is straight through.

In regard to negative emotions, one of my favorite college professors often said, "It's just pain; it won't kill you."[8] Experiencing heartache, rage, confusion, and despair is difficult. Fortunately, the human body is not designed to endure the brunt of these emotions for long. Sit with the pain, and it will eventually pass. It is important to note that not every child can handle this. Yet, under the right conditions, it may be exactly what is needed.

I once heard a pastor preach an entire sermon on Luke 2:1a. This simple passage states, "It came to pass."[5] The preacher focused on how difficulties come and go. This pastor has a good point; intense feelings do indeed "come to pass," which makes waiting things out a viable stress-relieving option.

The next set of ideas helps children to identify their emotions and sit with the pain. This way they can move on to a bright future on the other side—a future so bright that they may need to wear shades!

## Buster & Booster #58

Journal, and write your frustrations out.

## Buster & Booster #59

Name the feelings you are experiencing, and list possible reasons you feel this way.

> The simple act of verbalizing an emotion (or emotions) can bring clarity to the situation.

## Buster & Booster #60

Cry it out.

## Buster & Booster #61

Write a letter to the person you are upset with explaining why you are sad, angry, or frustrated, but don't send it.

> The point of this exercise is for children to gain a better understanding of how they feel in the moment. Once written, the letter can be read to a parent or to another trusted adult.

## Buster & Booster #62

Get creative by making a collage or sculpture of what you picture your anger, sadness, or frustration looks like.

## Buster & Booster #63

Watch a sad movie, and sit with the feeling.

Be sure to pick a happy activity to transition to after the movie is over. This coping skill works because it allows kids to experience an emotion for a set period and then moves them forward.

# CONNECT WITH OTHERS

Kids need community. Cookies are better with milk, fish cannot survive without water, and children require close connections to others. Psychologist Harry Harlow drove this point home in the 1950s with his infamous experiment with rhesus monkeys. In a University of Wisconsin laboratory, Dr. Harlow separated infant monkeys from their families. He then offered the tiny creatures a choice between two machine mothers instead.

Both surrogates were formed from wire mesh. The first provided food, while the second was wrapped in soft terrycloth to provide comfort. Surprisingly, the animals spent most of their time clinging to the terrycloth mother. By choosing nurture over the security of keeping food nearby, these mammals debunked the myth that relationships are a luxury.

In a second experiment, Harry divided the monkeys into two groups. The first had access to the terrycloth mother, while the second group was left on its own. Next, loud noises were introduced to examine how these animals would manage stress. The first group responded by clinging tightly to the terrycloth mother. The second group, lacking the presence of nurturing support, rocked back and forth, screeched loudly, clutched themselves tightly, and cowered in fear. Without a support system nearby, their stress skyrocketed.

Harry filmed his experiments, and they are heart-wrenching to watch. Nevertheless, these procedures are worth remembering because they demonstrate the profound need for warm, caring connections. Parents, teachers, pastors, friends, coaches, and mentors all play a vital role in helping kids to bust stress and boost their moods. The next strategies provide ideas for helping kids make the most of their support network and alleviate stress by closely connecting with others.

## Buster & Booster #64

Tell a safe friend how you feel.

> The key word is "safe." Every feeling should not be shared with everyone. Instead, adults can help kids identify a group of compassionate friends and supportive adults with whom they can closely connect.

## Buster & Booster #65

Phone a friend.

> This lifeline from the popular game show *Who Wants to Be a Millionaire* works just as well in everyday life.

## Buster & Booster #66

Ask for a hug.

## Buster & Booster #67

Hug a stuffed animal or a pillow.

> Dr. Harlow's experiment with rhesus monkeys demonstrates that when a caring human being is not around, a soft, cuddly surrogate will do.

## Buster & Booster #68

Talk to your parents or grandparents.

## Buster & Booster #69

Sit quietly with a friend.

## Buster & Booster #70

Send out a social media SOS.

> This strategy should be used with caution. For older kids who are active on social media, posting a broad message requesting support is quite the rage. Although less than ideal, when monitored by a wise adult, this can help kids connect.

## Buster & Booster #71

Schedule a time to talk to the most optimistic person you know.

## Buster & Booster #72

Browse through a photo album filled with happy memories.

> Some kids have difficulty recalling the good times and the positive people in their lives. When this is the case, creating a photo album

can help them internalize their friendships and happy times.

## Buster & Booster #73

Spend time with a pet.

## Buster & Booster #74

Talk to a therapist, mentor, Sunday school teacher, or life coach.

Because kids may need to hear the same wisdom from multiple adults before taking it to heart, enlisting the support of others often helps.

## Buster & Booster #75

Donate a toy to charity or to a child in need.

Supporting others is an excellent way to boost one's mood and often leads to developing positive relationships in the process.

71

## DISTRACT YOURSELF

Something that feels awful in the moment typically feels better a short time later. In my twenty-plus years of working with children, teens, and families, I have repeatedly found this to be true. After performing poorly on a test, thoughts of dropping out of school feel good. After arguing with a friend, ending the relationships feels like the right thing to do. And after cheating on a diet, bingeing for the remainder of the day feels best. *After all,* we say to ourselves, *since the diet is blown, I might as well enjoy the rest of the day.*

If any of these self-sabotaging behaviors sounds familiar, know that you are not alone. Although these illogical choices feel right, notice that *feels* is the key word. Because emotions change quickly, finding a distraction can prevent kids from making a rash decision that feels good in the moment but makes things worse in the future.

After an amygdala hijacking, it takes approximately twenty minutes for the frontal cortex to regain control. Even if a child appears calm, he or she may still not be in an optimal problem-solving state of mind. Fortunately, most difficulties don't need to be resolved immediately.

Wise adults might suggest, "You don't need to decide today. You can always give up, end the friendship, or make that bad choice tomorrow. For now, let's find something else to do." This next set of stress busters and mood boosters provides suggestions for helping kids step away from problems. Fortunately, disengaging—even for just a few moments—can make the world feel like a warmer place.

## Buster & Booster #76

Engross yourself in a maze, crossword puzzle, or dot-to-dot.

## Buster & Booster #77

Knit or weave.

## Buster & Booster #78

Pause and count to 10.

## Buster & Booster #79

Count backward from 100.

## Buster & Booster #80

Do a jigsaw puzzle.

## Buster & Booster #81

Garden.

## Buster & Booster #82

Paint.

## Buster & Booster #83

Bounce a balloon 100 times without letting it touch the floor.

If this is too easy, try it again using only your feet and knees to keep the balloon in the air.

## Buster & Booster #84

Pop Bubble Wrap.

This is a favorite for many kids.

## Buster & Booster #85

Sit by a lake, stream, or ocean.

## Buster & Booster #86

Read a book or comic book.

## Buster & Booster #87

Listen to an audiobook.

## ENGAGE THE SENSES

Some children respond especially well to sensory experiences. Just as each snowflake is unique, no two children are exactly alike. This is why psychology is an ongoing process of trial and error.

In my master's-level psychopharmacology class, I was surprised to learn that even when it comes to something as delicate as prescribing medication, psychiatry is still a combination of science and art. Psychiatrists understand which medications typically work best for each set of symptoms. Nevertheless, there are never any guarantees. Once a medication appears to be working, the dosage is refined. On the other hand, if the results are poor, then a new prescription is tried.

Similarly, therapists are well versed in helping their clients discover the therapeutic tools that work best for them. Parents, teachers, and supportive adults who want to help kids manage stress and increase their mood must undergo a similar process of trial and error. Some children respond especially well to sensory experiences, which is why this next set of ideas hones in on sight, sound, smell, taste, and textures. The best way to know if these strategies will work for your child is to try them.

## Buster & Booster #88

Rock in a rocking chair.

## Buster & Booster #89

Play with modeling clay.

## Buster & Booster #90

Smell a lemon or, better yet, make lemonade.

> The physical act of squeezing the lemons, combined with the vibrant smells, sweet taste of the sugar, and sour taste of the lemons all add to the sensory experience.

## Buster & Booster #91

Squeeze putty or let slime drip through your fingers.

## Buster & Booster #92

Crinkle tissue paper.

## Buster & Booster #93

Shake a glitter jar and watch the contents settle.

> Glitter jars are a hot parenting trend. To make your own, add glitter, glitter glue, food coloring, and water to a clear plastic water bottle. Be sure to fasten the cap on tightly. The more glitter glue added, the longer it will take the concoction to settle. Watching the swirling glitter is a soothing sensory experience. Some parents have their child shake the bottle and take a break until the glitter is resettled, which typically takes between one to three minutes.

## Buster & Booster #94

Finger paint.

## Buster & Booster #95

Wear cozy pajamas or socks.

## Buster & Booster #96

Wrap yourself in a warm blanket.

## Buster & Booster #97

Make cloud-dough.

> Do this by combining 8 cups of flour with 1 cup of baby oil. Have kids mix the concoction with their hands. Cloud-dough smells great and is fun to play with too!

## CHANGE YOUR SCENERY

A change of scenery is an excellent way to put problems back into their proper perspective. Shortly after graduating from college, I took up skydiving. Because of the high altitude of the jumps, the experience was more like floating than falling. The earth did not rush at me as expected. Instead, there was plenty of time to enjoy the view. As I gazed at the ocean, lakes, skyline, and stunning view below, problems melted away. The tiny bubble I lived in popped as I came face-to-face with the vastness, beauty, and awesomeness of our world!

Much to my dismay, I came to discover that purchasing my own parachute would cost more than paying off my car. This ended my stint of jumping out of airplanes. Of course, I am not suggesting that children go skydiving. There are plenty of safer and more cost-effective ways to assist kids in expanding their worldview. I share this story because most people can relate to getting caught up in a problem and then having an experience that jolts things back into perspective.

The human brain is adept at convincing kids that their challenges are massive. Changing their physical view can help them realize the universe is far bigger than the issues at hand. This next section provides ideas for encouraging kids to bust stress and boost their mood by altering their physical perspective.

## Buster & Booster #98

Do a downward dog pose.

## Buster & Booster #99

Do cartwheels or a handstand.

## Buster & Booster #100

Hang upside down from monkey bars, or lay upside down on the couch.

## Buster & Booster #101

Go for a bike or scooter ride.

## Buster & Booster #102

Climb a tree.

## Buster & Booster #103

Open the blinds.

## Buster & Booster #104

Open all the windows in your home.

> It is astounding what a little fresh air can do.

## Buster & Booster #105

Spend time outside.

## Buster & Booster #106

Volunteer at a soup kitchen or homeless shelter.

> Supporting others in need is a superb way of helping kids keep their problems in proper perspective.

## Buster & Booster #107

Go outside, lie on a blanket, and look up at the clouds.

## Buster & Booster #108

Go for a walk at night, and gaze at the stars.

> Try to identify constellations and search for shooting stars. To make this activity even more meaningful, spend a few moments researching the size of the universe in an encyclopedia or on the internet first. This can help kids grasp the magnitude of what they observe during their stargazing adventure.

## CHANGE YOUR MENTAL VIEW

"There is nothing either good or bad, but thinking makes it so." This well-known quote from Shakespeare's *Hamlet* speaks to the power of changing one's mental outlook. As I stated earlier, Albert Ellis, the founder of Rational Emotive Behavior Therapy, used the terms *awfulizing* and *catastrophizing* to describe how focusing on a problem magnifies it. Michel de Montaigne said, "My life has been filled with terrible misfortune, most of which never happened." Sadly, many kids can say the same.

The good news is that changing one's mental perspective can pull kids out of this rut. This next set of stress busters and mood boosters focuses on thought-changing strategies that work especially well for children. Because each one requires some additional explanation, this section is longer than the previous ones. Yet these are some of my favorite tools, and learning them is worth the additional effort.

## Buster & Booster #109

Squash ANTs.

> ANTs is an acronym for automatic negative thoughts. Ants are annoying creatures that march into our homes, and ANTs are intrusive thoughts that invade our kids' minds. The solution is to recognize these buggers before they make mountains out of molehills. Then squash them by replacing the negative thoughts with more rational, positive ones.

## Buster & Booster #110

Reframe the problem.

> Have you noticed how a picture that does not look quite right suddenly fits nicely after the frame is changed? Mental reframing is similar. A problem viewed as "awful" can be reframed as an "adventure," "an opportunity for growth," or "a normal part of growing up." The next set of stress busters and mood boosters contains some of my favorite reframes. Of course, you can always create your own too.

## Buster & Booster #111

Tell yourself: *This is an adventure.*

> Instead of viewing struggles as a catastrophe, decide they are an adventure. After all, it is likely you will make new friends, develop valuable skills, and make fascinating discoveries along the way.

## Buster & Booster #112

Tell yourself: *This is a learning experience and an opportunity for growth.*

> Failing a test, losing a friendship, or coming in last place does not have to lead to despair. Children can use the experience as an opportunity for growth, choosing to fail forward instead. After all, most childhood blunders are fairly easy to bounce back from, making this the ideal time for mistakes.

## Buster & Booster #113

Tell yourself: *I am a survivor.*

Kids can decide not to be a victim and choose to view themselves as a survivor instead. This is an excellent reframe for children who have experienced trauma. The bright side is that children are resilient. I like this reframe because it takes the spotlight off tragedy and places it on one's ability to bounce back stronger and wiser than ever before.

## Buster & Booster #114

Tell yourself: *This is a good story that will help a lot of people one day.*

I like this reframe because it hones in on how a challenging story can be used to inspire others.

## Buster & Booster #115

Tell yourself: *It is an experiment.* Then, get curious about the results.

> I love the classic picture of the mad scientist holding a beaker in each hand. There is usually a mischievous smile on his face because this scientist knows he is about to make an important discovery. He may find a formula that turns lead into gold, or the concoction could explode. Either way, once the beakers are mixed, this scientist will be a little bit wiser. Instead of stressing, help children adopt the mad scientist attitude. View new endeavors as an experiment. Then, grow from the results.

## Buster & Booster #116

Identify ways that life is unfair to your advantage.

> "Life is not fair." This is a concept that adults frequently attempt to pass on to kids. The implication is "You better learn to deal with difficulties because life is unfairly against you." However, life can also be unfair in a child's favor. For example, living in the

United States (one of the wealthiest and freest nations on earth) and having good health and a loving family are all undeserved blessings. Adults can help children boost their mood by encouraging them to identify ways that life is unfair to their advantage.

## Buster & Booster #117

Use softer language when describing negative events.

A primary concept of Neural Linguistic Programming, or NLP for short, is that feelings are connected to language. When kids describe their circumstances as "horrible" or "terrible," their mood adjusts to fit this intensity. On the other hand, when softer language is employed, by using words like "disappointing" or "mildly frustrating," the emotional impact is lessened. NLP does not suggest that kids should pretend the world is all rainbows and unicorns. Instead, it promotes reducing the emotional impact of negative events by softening one's language.

## Buster & Booster #118

Get energized by using power words to describe positive life events.

> On a similar note, NLP teaches that words also energize. Tell a child, "You did well," and he or she will smile. Proclaim, "You studied hard for that test and did awesome!" and that child's face will light up. Words tell our brain how to feel. Using vibrant, uplifting language will not only cause you to feel empowered but soon the kids around you will follow suit.

## Buster & Booster #119

Embrace your imperfections, rough edges, and mistakes by being thankful for them.

> Imperfect people connect best with other imperfect people. On the one hand, nonstick pans are excellent cooking utensils, because their smooth coating allows burned foods to slide right off. On the other hand, a smooth coating is less desirable for human beings. Kids need to know that rough edges, failures, and humanness are what allow relationships

to stick. Therefore, instead of hiding imperfections, embrace them. Admittedly, this is a big concept for children to grasp. Yet it is never too early to begin teaching this invaluable mood-boosting lesson.

## PRACTICE GOOD SELF-TALK

People tell themselves how to act and what to feel. If you don't believe me, try this experiment. The next time you feel down, attempt to identify the specific thoughts running through your mind. Chances are they are negative and self-defeating. These thoughts may include statements like:

- *This is too hard.*

- *I will never figure it out.*

- *Someone else would be better at this than I would.*

Kids use this type of negative self-talk all the time. Adults can help kids bust stress and boost their mood by teaching them simple self-talk statements to use throughout the day. One way to accomplish this is by repeating these phrases aloud at opportune times.

I had a professor do this in college. Then one day, when it felt like I would never reach the graduation finish line, one of his famous phrases popped into my head. I was surprised to find that my self-talk contained this professor's exact tone and inflections. It was as if he was standing right next to me.

This wise psychology professor had gotten inside my head, and it was just what I needed to continue pressing forward. In this section, you will find some of my favorite self-talk statements for kids. Feel free to use the ones I provide or create your own.

## Buster & Booster #120

Tell yourself, *Go slow, be patient, and take your time.*

> Kids increase their troubles by reacting too quickly. Most problems do not need to be resolved right now, and trying only generates additional chaos. When emotions run high, one of the best things children can do is to remind themselves to go slow, be patient, and take their time. In the classic story of "The Tortoise and the Hare," the tortoise wins every time. Slow and steady is a recipe for winning in countless areas of life.

## Buster & Booster #121

Tell yourself, *Oops, maybe next time.*

> This self-talk statement reminds kids to view errors as fixable. In fact, childhood is one of the best times to make mistakes because kids nearly always have another opportunity to get things right.

## Buster & Booster #122

Remind yourself, *Trust the process.*

> Doing the work leads to achieving the goal. This self-talk statement reminds kids to complete what they are asked to do without protest, trusting that the process will lead them to what they desire. "Trust the process" is the phrase that inspired me to keep pressing forward when I was discouraged, so I know the power of this simple statement.

## PRACTICE SELF-CARE

Self-care energizes us so we can encourage others. My first car was a 1987 Suzuki Swift. Although this two-door, four-seat hatchback was a tight fit for my six-foot frame, I did not mind. For me, this car equaled freedom. Then one day, the car wouldn't start. Unsure of what to do next, I walked into the house to think. When I returned, the engine fired right up. *Did I simply imagine my car not starting?* I wondered to myself.

A week later, the problem resurfaced. After turning the key in the ignition, the engine remained silent. As a naive college student, I decided the best course of action was to ignore the issue for the second time. When I returned a short time later, the engine once again effortlessly ignited.

This ridiculous routine went on for some months. Since I was ultimately able to get to where I wanted to go, I figured I could live with the delays. My only real concern was that each week the condition grew worse.

Eventually, I decided to take my car to a mechanic. It turns out the vehicle had a bad starter. The mechanic explained that the problem would escalate until the part was replaced. Understanding this finally caused me to take action. With a fresh starter, the engine ignited with every turn of the key.

Some kids treat their physical bodies similar to the way I treated my first car. They stay up late, eat far too much junk food, and don't practice good personal hygiene. This leads to lethargy and difficulties appearing bigger than they are. In other words, these kids have starter problems and, as I did, are choosing to ignore them. Unfortunately, this lack of appropriate self-care leads to decreased energy, enthusiasm, and get-up-and-go.

Contrary to popular belief, self-care is not selfish. Instead, it energizes kids so they can encourage others. I love walking into our home at the end of the day. No matter how challenging my day has been, hearing my four girls squeal with delight, "Daddy is home," always renews my joy. Yet, energizing others is only possible when kids take care of themselves first.

As in previous sections, many of these stress-busting and mood-boosting strategies are common sense. Nevertheless, they are included in this book because children often fail to practice the invaluable skills they already know. This next section provides self-care strategies to help kids reduce stress and feel better about themselves so they can refresh others.

## Buster & Booster #123

Eat a healthy snack—especially if you are hangry.

> "Hangry," or hungry-angry, is a new expression that acknowledges that one's appetite is connected to his or her mood. Not all kids recognize their body's signals. Adults can help kids boost their mood by assisting them in identifying and meeting their physical needs.

## Buster & Booster #124

Go to bed early and sleep on it.

> When it comes to resolving problems, very little good happens after 8 p.m. I share this wisdom with parents, and Jenny and I readily apply it in our own home. Yet there is a delicate balance to this. On the one hand, bedtime is when children are most ready to

talk, making evenings an excellent time to learn about their day. On the other hand, nighttime is also when problem-solving is the most difficult. If you catch your child growing increasingly emotional, don't be afraid to say, "Honey, why don't you get some sleep. We can talk more in the morning." It is truly astounding how a good night's rest can improve a child's entire outlook on life.

## Buster & Booster #125

Get a haircut, trim your nails, or get a pedicure.

## Buster & Booster #126

Start each day by making your bed.

In his bestselling book, *Make Your Bed: Little Things That Can Change Your Life. . . And Maybe Even the World*,[9] William McRaven suggests that beginning each day by completing a small task with excellence— such as making one's bed—sets a tone of excellence for the remainder of the day. This simple idea is pure genius and worth passing on to kids.

## Buster & Booster #127

Say no.

This is also known as setting good boundaries. Because kids have more options than ever before, they must become adept at saying no. Otherwise, all the available selections can overwhelm them. In our home, Jenny and I teach our kids to say no to some good things, to make time to say yes to great opportunities that come their way.

## CHOOSE WISELY

Happy kids focus on how they can improve their situation, as opposed to trying to get what they want by beguiling others. William Glasser, the founder of Choice Theory, refers to attempts to control, bribe, and manipulate others as *external control psychology*. According to Glasser, external control psychology does not work because it always harms the relationship, and relationship problems are at the root of nearly all human miseries.

Glasser's solution is simple. Instead of attempting to change others, focus on the positive choices you can make instead. My third-grade teacher proclaimed, "When you point the finger at someone else, you have three fingers pointing back at you." This is Glasser's wisdom stated at a child's level. Children are not helpless, and most kids have more options than they realize. This next set of strategies inspires children to bust stress and boost their mood by taking their eyes off others and focusing on the choices they can make.

## Buster & Booster #128

Decide on the best course of action by creating a pros-and-cons list.

> This simple but powerful tool can help children make wise choices when deciding is difficult. Start by folding a sheet of notebook paper in half. Then write the pros of the decision on one side and the cons on the other. Looking at a decision from this perspective can provide clarity on what to do next.

## Buster & Booster #129

Take one small step toward resolving the problem.

> The purpose of this strategy is to build momentum. Without momentum, making progress feels like wading through a swimming pool full of cold, sticky syrup—advancement is slow and gaining headway requires a great deal of effort. However, once momentum is in our kid's favor, progress feels like a downhill sled ride. Adults can help kids build momentum by assisting them

101

in breaking down their goals into small, actionable steps. Then encourage them to reach their goal one small step at a time.

## Buster & Booster #130

Forgive.

It is said that unforgiveness is like drinking poison and hoping the other person feels sick. In other words, when kids hold on to past hurts, they injure themselves the most. Adults can help kids boost their happiness by teaching them to let go, forgive, and move on.

## MOOD-BOOSTER STACKING

After practicing the basic ideas in this book, kids can level up their stress-busting and mood-boosting abilities by stacking their favorite strategies together. While reading this book, perhaps you have found yourself thinking, *I have tried these strategies before, and they don't work.* Unfortunately, raising kids—even extraordinarily good kids—requires hard labor and intentional effort.

The good news is that there is always something new to try, which is one of the reasons for including so many ideas in this book. However, if you still find yourself discouraged, then it may be time for the next steps.

First, understand that change is difficult. More often than not, bad habits form over a period of months or years, which mean they will take significant time to break. Growth most often occurs in small spurts, with periods of regression along the way. If this is true in your family, then congratulations, you are normal. A patient persistence, coupled with an enthusiastic belief that change is possible, is a powerful ally on this journey.

So keep practicing these skills with your kids, and continue pressing forward.

Second, although most of the stress busters and mood boosters in this book are simple, know that helping your kids learn them is only the beginning. The next step is to practice stacking these skills together. A child might do this by taking a deep breath, walking away from a negative situation, changing his or her self-talk using one of the phrases provided, and then going for a brisk walk to burn off any excess frustration. This is an example of using four strategies in tandem, and it produces a dynamic mood-boosting effect!

## Buster & Booster #131

Stack your favorite strategies together to build massive stress-busting, mood-boosting momentum.

# Helping Kids Fully Recharge

Gracefully navigating stressful situations is easiest when kids are already in a positive mood. Have you ever woken up from a full night's rest feeling rejuvenated and indomitable—as if you could conquer any difficulty that comes your way? If so, then you probably already understand the value of the advice in this chapter.

Although coping skills are an excellent way for kids to bust stress and boost their mood in the moment, children also require longer breaks to recharge fully. Not long ago, I stepped out of the hustle and bustle of my standard routine, and this break reminded me of the significance of unmitigated downtime.

After spending nearly twenty hours tied to a tree in an isolated patch of snow-covered forest, I feel great. My thoughts are clear. My mind is bursting with fresh ideas. Everything around me seems vivid and alive. *I can't wait to do this again next year,* I enthusiastically think to myself.

My father-in-law calls this experience hunting, and technically, I wasn't tied to a tree but clipped into a deer stand fifteen feet above the woodland floor. Nevertheless, for the majority of that weekend, a lone tree was my abode. When I returned home, my wife, Jenny, who was raised in Minnesota and is used to the deer-hunting obsession, declared, "I don't get it. What draws guys to hunting?"

Of course, there was a time when hunting was done out of pure necessity. Providing for one's family entailed killing something and dragging it home. However, today, with grocery stores in every city and fast-food restaurants on most corners, this need no longer exists.

For me, one major draw is tranquility. Uninterrupted stillness is a rare commodity. In fact, it is so rare that the first few hours alone with my thoughts were difficult. Then the magic happened. As I sat in the incessant stillness, I could almost feel my body recharging. In a world of frenzied movement, hunting became my excuse to be still.

## THINKING HOLIDAYS

A therapist I know tells the story of a family friend who went through an especially challenging time in his life. The friend reported that he stopped taking his prescribed medication because the drugs made it difficult to think. After a particularly stressful day, this man reached his breaking point and began acting in ways that were drastically out of character. Fortunately, my therapist friend was nearby and suggested this man permit himself to take a thinking holiday. After this conversation, the man checked himself into a hospital and resumed his prescribed medication.

👍 👍 👍

Although this story is an extreme example, I share it because all of us need an occasional thinking holiday. This is true for both adults and kids. Whether the break comes in the form of a day off from school, an extended vacation, or a weekend hunting excursion, finding longer ways to regenerate is crucial.

## DISCOVERING YOUR CHILD'S TREE

What is your child's tree? How does he or she step out of the hustle and bustle of life to recharge? These are important questions to ask because coping skills are less potent if your child is continually running near empty. It may be helpful to picture coping skills as a daily multivitamin that alleviates but does not cure. If it has been an especially stressful year, taking additional time to recuperate before implementing the ideas in this book may be warranted.

## BUSTING STRESS IN A CHANGING WORLD

In my previous book, *131 Boredom Busters and Creativity Builders for Kids,* I share our family's journey from overly entertained and hyper-scheduled to finding a more balanced approach to life. In 2014, some articles were published referring to the micro-generation born between 1977 and 1983 as Xennials. Since this is my generation, the term caught my eye, and the articles reminded me how quickly the world changes. Xennials are "the last kids to make it all the way to grown up without pervasive technology."[10]

For today's children, smartphones, laptops, and wireless internet are the norm. Of course, as society progresses, strategies for helping kids bust stress and boost their mood must advance too. The days when parents had to seek out activities for their children are long gone. Today, it is a matter of deciding which sports, hobbies, and interests our children will join, out of a multitude of options available. While this progress is not bad, adults need to be aware that kids are growing up in a far different world than they remember.

## A WORLD WITHOUT WALLS

In middle school, I heard a speaker relay the following story:

> Growing up is like traversing down a narrow hallway. When my generation were kids, the hallway doors were closed, and most were locked. My friends and I would occasionally hear other children talk about sex, alcohol, drugs, and engaging in other subversive activities. However, most of these things were not easily accessible. For your generation, it is as if the doors of this hallway are unlocked and cracked open. Dangers and pitfalls are more readily available to you than they were for me.

If this was true for my generation, then our kids have the doors, and perhaps even the walls, of this hallway removed entirely. Open internet access and broader access to information in general put a wealth of knowledge at our kids' fingertips. As with most changes, these advances have both their pros and cons. The aim is not to build fear but to create awareness. Because the world is continually changing, adults need to adapt in the ways they support kids in managing stress.

## PRACTICE MAKES PERFECT

Stress-busting, mood-boosting skills are more likely to be caught than taught. If you begin by regulating your own emotions, the kids around you will begin to follow your example. Although this book is written specifically for parents and educators who desire to assist children in self-regulating, these ideas work for adults too. In fact, when I present these strategies to families, parents often state, "I think all of us will benefit from this."

## IN THIS TOGETHER

You and I are on this journey of equipping our children, with a host of other parents, teachers, and mentors. So be encouraged, knowing that you are not alone. Helping children learn to exert effortful control over their emotions is indeed an ongoing process. As my former college professor, Dr. Lord, would say, "Trust the process." Start by teaching these skills to your children. Then model and practice them daily. Finally, reinforce progress with hearty praise every time you catch a child putting one of these skills into action.

As we have seen, healthy relationships, career success, and overall happiness are tied to a child's ability to manage his or her emotions. In short, self-regulating kids possess greater odds of excelling virtually everywhere. So keep pressing forward, because the rewards are worth the effort. I continue to wish you and the kids in your care much success in this ongoing stress-busting and mood-boosting journey!

# End Notes

1.  James Clear, "40 Years of Stanford Research Found That People With This One Quality Are More Likely to Succeed," James Clear, accessed January 1, 2018 https://jamesclear.com/delayed-gratification.
2.  "The Marshmallow Test," YouTube, last modified September 24, 2009, https://www.youtube.com/watch?v=QX_oy96 14HQ.
3.  Robert L. Leahy, *The Worry Cure: Seven Steps to Stop Worry from Stopping You* (New York: Harmony, 2005).
4.  David G. Myers, *Psychology*, 9th ed. (New York: Worth, 2010).
5.  Scripture quoted by permission. All scripture quotations, unless otherwise indicated, are taken from the NET Bible® copyright ©1996-2017 by Biblical Studies Press, L.L.C. All rights reserved.
6.  Robert Emmons and Michael McCullough, "Highlights from the Research Project on Gratitude and Thankfulness, accessed January 1, 2018, http://citeseerx.ist.psu.edu/viewdoc/download ?doi=10.1.1.520.4351&rep=rep1&type=pdf.

7. Jonathan Silverstine, "Tickle Me Elmos Selling for $5,000," ABC News, published October 19, 2006, http://abcnews.go.com/Technology/story?id=2583572&page=1%0c

8. Quote attributed to Dr. Barry Lord, quoted from this author's memory.

9. William McRaven, *Make Your Bed: Little Things That Can Change Your Life... And Maybe Even the World* (New York: Grand Central, 2017).

10. Trisha Leigh Zeigenhorn, "There's Now a Name for the Micro Generation Born Between 1977-1983" *Did You Know?*, last modified June 27, 2017, http://didyouknowfacts.com/theres-now-a-name-for-the-micro-generation-born-between-1977-1983/

# Thumbs Up or Thumbs Down

Thank you for purchasing this book!

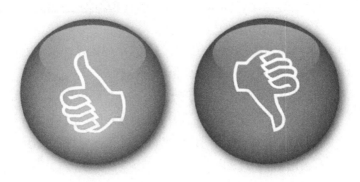

I would love to hear from you. Your feedback not only helps me grow as a writer but it also helps me get books into the hands of those who need them most. Online reviews are one of the biggest ways that independent authors—like me—connect with new readers.

If you loved the book, could you please share your experience? Leaving feedback is as easy as answering any of these questions:

- What did you like about the book?

- What is your most important takeaway or insight?

- What have you done differently—or what will you do differently because of what you have read?

- To whom would you recommend this book?

Of course, I am looking for honest reviews. So if you have a minute to share your experience, good or bad, please consider leaving a review!

I look forward to hearing from you!

Sincerely,

COFFEE SHOP CONVERSATIONS

# About the Author

Jed is passionate about helping people live happier, healthier, more connected lives by having better conversations. He is a husband, a father of four girls, a psychology professor, therapist, and writer.

Jed graduated from Southern California Seminary with a master of divinity and returned to complete a second master's degree in psychology. In his free time, Jed enjoys walking on the beach, reading, and spending time with his incredible family.

If you enjoyed this book, I would love it if you would leave a review. Your feedback is an awesome encouragement to me, and it helps books like this one get noticed. It only takes a minute, and every review is greatly appreciated. Oh, and please feel free to stay in touch too!

Email: jed@coffeeshopconversations.com

Twitter: @jjurchenko

Facebook: Coffee Shop Conversations

Blog: www.CoffeeShopConversations.com

# More Family Books

This book and other creative conversation starters are available at www.Amazon.com.

Transform your relationship from dull and bland to inspired, passionate, and connected as you grow your insights into your partner's inner world! Whether you are newly dating or nearing your golden anniversary, these questions are for you. This book will help you share your heart and better know your partner.

**131 Creative Conversations for Couples**

These creative conversation starters will inspire your kids to pause their electronics, grow their social skills, and develop lifelong relationships!

This book is for children and tweens who desire to build face-to-face connections and everyone who wants to help their kids connect in an increasingly disconnected world. Get your kids talking with this activity book the entire family will enjoy.

**131 Conversations That Engage Kids**

Made in the USA
Coppell, TX
26 March 2020

17759070R00066